MW00915321

100 Practical English Phrasal Verbs

By Alex Makar

EnglishAlex.com

EnglishAlex.com

Copyright ©2020 Alex Makar.

All rights reserved. No part of this publication may be reproduced, distributed, or transmitted in any form or by any means, including photocopying, recording, or other electronic or mechanical methods, without the prior written permission of the publisher, except in the case of brief quotations embodied in critical reviews and certain other noncommercial uses permitted by copyright law. For permission requests, write to the publisher, addressed "Attention: Permissions Coordinator," at the email address below.

Front cover image and book design by Maggie Makar.

First printing edition 2020.

alex@englishalex.com
EnglishAlex.com

Dedicated to everyone affected by the COVID-19 pandemic. May we learn our lessons and return to the world kinder, stronger, and wiser.

Table of Contents

Table of Contents

Author's Note

Thank you for purchasing *100 Practical English Phrasal Verbs*. This book is the product of over ten years of English teaching experience. It is a reference guide intended for self-study or classroom study, and it was written with English students and teachers in mind.

The name *100 Practical English Phrasal Verbs* was chosen with the belief that second language learners need clear and useful vocabulary to develop their skills and confidence. With that in mind, I have chosen to focus on one hundred of the most common English phrasal verbs with only the most modern definitions and usages. You will not find definitions that are only relevant to a particular past decade or century in these pages, nor ones that have a low rate of use. My goal is for this book to be useful no matter which definition or example a student opens up to, and for it to remain relevant for many years to come.

Finally, I'd like to give some special thank yous: to my wife and children for their love, patience, and support as I typed this at the kitchen table, on the living room couch, or alone in the basement, taking time away from them so I could pursue a personal dream; to my parents, for making sure we had what we needed, and to my sisters, for the laughs and Nintendo sessions; to my sister Maggie Makar for making this book look as good as it does with her design skills; to the administrative team at engvid.com for believing in me and allowing me to have a platform to teach English to the world since 2009; to every student I have ever taught, whether in person or through a screen, for their trust and kindness; and finally, to every teacher, friend, and colleague I have ever come across for contributing to and sharing in this journey. In the wise words of Marcus Aurelius, "Accept the things to which fate binds you, and love the people with whom fate brings you together."

Alex Makar
April 23rd, 2020

Introduction

How to use this book
You can use this book either as a reference for learning phrasal verbs that you have read or heard in daily life (scan the index for this approach,) or as a structured guide for learning a few phrasal verbs at a time. I recommend doing one lesson every two or three days if you want to use the second approach. The lessons gradually increase in difficulty.

What is a phrasal verb?
A phrasal verb is an idiomatic expression that consists of at least two parts, most commonly: a verb and an adverb (look up,) a verb and a preposition (come across,) or both (come up with.) There are rare exceptions to these structures (take care of,) but the vast majority of phrasal verbs fall into one of these types.

A phrasal verb can have multiple meanings

Example:

"Hold on a minute."   (Wait a minute.)

"They held on for the win."   (They persevered and
                                       managed to be successful
                                       despite difficulties.)

Phrasal verbs can be transitive or intransitive

Transitive phrasal verbs

- **Need a <u>direct object</u> to act on.**
  Example: Put on
  "Put on <u>your shoes</u>." (shoes are the object.)
  "~~Put on!~~" (not possible. Object needed.)

- **The majority can be separated.**
  Example: Take off
  "Take off <u>your jacket</u>." = "Take <u>your jacket</u> off."

- **Can use an object pronoun in the middle of a separable phrasal verb, but can't use one at the end of any phrasal verb.**
  Example: Turn off
  "Turn <u>it</u> off." "~~Turn off it.~~"

- **Some can't be separated.**
  Example: Look after
  "Look after <u>Daniel</u>." "~~Look Daniel after.~~"

- **Some must be separated depending on usage.**
  Example: Get out
  "I got <u>Bo</u> out." (I helped Bo to leave a place or bad situation.)
  "~~I got out Bo.~~" (possible if the intended usage is to remove something named Bo from a bag.)

Intransitive phrasal verbs

- **Have no direct object and are able to stand on their own.**
  Example: Get up
  When do you <u>get up</u>?"
  "~~Get up the baby.~~"

Some phrasal verbs can be both transitive and intransitive

Example: Clean up

"I cleaned up."

"I cleaned up my room."

What's the best way to learn phrasal verbs?

The best way to learn phrasal verbs, and vocabulary in general, is through context. This means seeing or hearing a new phrasal verb in a book, movie, or real life conversation, finding out what it means, and then trying to use it yourself.

Of course, for those who want to be more proactive about learning phrasal verbs, you can continue context-based learning by reading a book like this one. This book promotes learning through context in four ways:

1. By grouping phrasal verbs together which have direct opposites (ex. turn on and turn off.)

2. By grouping phrasal verbs together which are similar in meaning and can therefore be used in similar contexts (ex. throw away, throw out, and get rid of.)

3. By including four example sentences for the most common usage of each phrasal verb, and two example sentences for other usages.

4. By including a common sentence at the end of each phrasal verb entry and explaining its meaning in plain language.

In the end, you must find the approach that works best for you.

Good luck!

Lesson 1

wake up, get up, open up, sit down, stand up

Wake up

1. **to wake; to open your eyes and become alert after sleeping**

transitive or intransitive, separable
common extensions: wake up at/on/in a particular time/day/period of time/etc.

"My brother has a hard time waking up in the morning."

"She's been asleep for over eleven hours. Should we wake her up?"

"When did you wake up today?"

"Wake up! We're going to be late!"

2. **to become alert and active after a period of laziness, fatigue, or inactivity**

transitive or intransitive, separable

"I need coffee to wake me up in the morning."

"He exercises every morning to help himself wake up."

3. **to start paying more attention to something; to become aware of a situation or reality**

transitive or intransitive, separable
common extension: wake up to something

"That documentary really woke me up to the dangers of fast food."

"You need to wake up to the truth; you deserve to be here as much as anyone else."

common sentence: "Wake up!" (Imperative used to tell someone to stop sleeping. Often said by family members and roommates. Could also be used to tell someone to start paying better attention to something.)

Get up

1. to leave your bed after sleeping (also: get out of bed)

intransitive
common extensions: get up at/on/in a particular time/day/period of time/etc.

"When do you usually get up in the morning?"

"We got up really late yesterday."

"I'm going to try to get up by 7AM."

"Mark always gets up early."

2. to rise to a standing position after sitting or lying down (similar: stand up)

transitive or intransitive, separable (common: get someone up)

"Get him up off the floor!"

"You'd better get up if you don't want to have back problems after sitting for so long."

3. to ascend or cause to ascend

transitive or intransitive, separable

"Get up those stairs right now! It's bath time and I don't want to argue!"

"We need to get this refrigerator up to the third floor."

common sentence: "When do you get up in the morning?" (What time do you wake up and leave your bed in the morning?)

Open up

1. to open (a door, window, store, etc.)

transitive or intransitive, separable

"Could you open up the window? It's a bit warm in here."

"I opened the bag up and discovered it was empty."

"What time does the store open up?"

"Open up! It's me!" (while knocking on a door)

2. to create a new opportunity or possibility

transitive or intransitive, separable

"Learning a second language would open up new possibilities for you."

"Putting your business online opens the world up to you."

3. to make it easier or possible to travel to or do business in a particular region, usually in official contexts

transitive or intransitive, separable

"They've been talking about opening up their travel laws again."

"This new foreign policy will open things up for international investors."

common sentence: "Police! Open up!" (Often used in police crime dramas. You can also use "Open up!" in your daily life if you're knocking on someone's door and want the person to open the door quickly.)

Sit down

1. to sit

intransitive
common extensions: sit down at/on/in something, or with someone

"Thanks for coming. You can sit down wherever you like."

"Sit down. You're making me nervous just standing there."

"We all sat down at the dinner table."

"Do we have enough chairs for everyone to sit down on?"

2. to make someone sit

transitive, must be separated (sit someone down)
common extensions: sit someone down at/on/in something, or with someone

"I sat him down because he looked dizzy."

"Sit your butt down!" (said in anger to someone you are reprimanding)

common sentence: "Sit down and relax." (A casual imperative telling someone to sit and relax. Often used after inviting someone into your home. Also common: "Have a seat" or "Take a seat.")

Stand up

1. to stand; to rise from a seated or lying position
intransitive

"He stood up and offered the pregnant woman his seat on the bus."

"You should stand up. You've been sitting at your desk for three hours."

"Could you help me to stand up? I'm not as young as I used to be."

"Ouch! That looked like it hurt. Are you able to stand up?"

2. to make someone stand
transitive, must be separated (stand someone up)

"Stand your brother up. He's being dramatic and lying on the floor."

"She looks hurt. Should we try to stand her up?"

3. not meeting someone you had previously arranged to meet, and not telling them about the cancelation (usually someone you are dating)
transitive, usually separated (stand someone up)

"I can't believe he stood you up at the restaurant!"

"I waited for her for an hour before I realized she had stood me up."

4. to defend yourself verbally
transitive, inseparable (stand up for yourself)

"Are you going to let him call you lazy? Stand up for yourself!"

"I was so proud to see her stand up for herself against her father." (also: "I was so proud to see her stand up to her father!")

5. to react with strength to certain conditions or treatment

transitive, inseparable (stand up to something)

"I'm not sure if that fence is strong enough to stand up to strong winds."

"Our community needs to stand up to bullying."

common sentence: "Stand up for yourself." (Speak and defend yourself. Do not let others define your identity for you or talk negatively about you. Usually said to support and/or encourage a friend.)

Lesson 2

turn on, turn off, turn up, turn down, hurry up

Turn on

1. to activate (usually a machine, switch, or device, but can be figurative)
transitive or intransitive, separable

"Could you turn on the air conditioner/TV/radio/laptop/heater/etc.?"

"Could you turn the lights on, please?"

"He always turns on the charm when he's around new clients."

"Come on, Marty. Are you even listening? Did you forget to turn your brain on this morning?"

2. to make someone feel sexually aroused
transitive or intransitive, separable

"Are you turned on right now?"

"That perfume is really turning me on."

3. to suddenly change your attitude and become aggressive towards someone; to attack or speak angrily to someone
transitive, inseparable (turn on someone)

"We were having a normal conversation when he suddenly turned on me!"

"They turned on each other after ten years of friendship."

common sentence: "Could you turn on the light(s)?" (Could you activate the light(s) in this room? A common request.)

Turn off

1. to deactivate (usually a machine, switch, or device, but can be figurative)
transitive or intransitive, separable

"Did you remember to turn off the stove?"

"Don't forget to turn off the alarm system."

"He's incapable of turning his anger off once it's on."

"Did you remember to turn the light off in the bathroom?"

2. to make someone lose interest in something
transitive, separable (usually separated: turn someone off)

"I really like this TV, but the price really turns me off."

"The car is nice, but the automatic transmission kind of turns me off."

3. to prevent or stop someone from feeling sexually attracted to you; to repel someone (usually with a bad habit, unattractive action or character)
transitive or intransitive, separable

"Smoking really turns me off."

"The date was going well, but I got turned off when he started chewing with his mouth open."

4. to leave or turn from one road or path and start going down another
transitive or intransitive, inseparable
common extension: turn off at a particular highway exit

"I'm going to turn off at the next exit. I need a bathroom break."

"Why did you turn off Main Street? This isn't the right way."

common sentence: "Turn it off." (Deactivate it. A common request.)

Turn up

1. to increase the intensity of something by adjusting the controls
transitive, separable

"Would you mind turning up the heat?"

"I can't hear anything. Could you turn up the volume?"

"Turn the radio up! I love this song!" (increase the volume of the radio)

"You're sweating. I'll turn the air conditioning up a bit."

2. to arrive unexpectedly or after people have waited for a long time
intransitive

"Did you hear that Jason turned up at Jessie's birthday?"

"Lisa! I'm so glad you turned up!"

3. to find or discover something unexpected, lost, or hidden; to be found or discovered after being lost or not known about
transitive or intransitive, separable

"The victim's body turned up two days after the 911 call."

"The research I did didn't turn anything up."

4. to happen, usually by chance or accident
intransitive

"Don't stop looking for a new job. I'm sure something will turn up soon."

"Has anything new turned up since the last time I talked to you?"

common sentence: "I'm sure something will turn up." (I'm sure something will happen and/or you will find what you are looking for soon. Often said to someone who is looking for a job.)

Turn down

1. to decrease the intensity of something by adjusting the controls
transitive, separable

"You're going to burn the sauce. Turn down the heat on the stove."

"The TV is too loud. Could you turn it down?"

"This game is too hard. I'm going to turn down the difficulty level."

"My computer's not powerful enough to handle this video. I'm going to turn down the resolution."

2. to refuse an offer, request, invitation, or person
transitive, separable

"He asked me out on a date, but I turned him down."

"The salary is very tempting, but I have to turn the promotion down."

common sentence: "Could you turn it down a bit?" (Could you lower the intensity a little? Usually said about the volume of a TV, radio, etc.)

Hurry up

1. to hurry; to do something more quickly
intransitive
common extension: hurry up with

"We'd better hurry up if we don't want to be late."

"Hurry up! The bus leaves in two minutes!"

"I wish this website would hurry up and load already. It's so slow!"

"Could you ask your brother to hurry up with the car? We need to leave right away."

2. **to make someone hurry; to make someone do something more quickly**

transitive, separable (usually separated: hurry someone up)

"If you don't hurry her up a bit, we're all going to miss the show."

"Is there any way to hurry up this printer?"

common sentence: "Hurry up already!" (Do what you are doing more quickly. I am getting impatient and/or we do not have a lot of time.)

Lesson 3

put on, take off, pick up, put down, drop off

Put on

1. **to place something on your body in order to wear it**
transitive, separable

"Put your jacket on."

"Do you need help putting your shoes on?"

"It's cold outside. You should put on a hat."

"I'd put on a scarf if I were you."

2. **to organize and/or perform a show, exhibition, concert, etc.**
transitive, separable

"My brother's theatre company puts on performances every weekend."

"I've never seen Metallica live, but I've heard they put on a good show."

3. **to become heavier; to gain weight and/or muscle**
transitive, separable

"He's trying to put on another ten pounds of muscle."

"We both put weight on after we got married."

4. **to activate something by pushing a button, pulling a lever, etc. (also: turn on)**
transitive, separable

"Have you put the washing machine on yet?"

"Remember to put the nightlight on in the hallway before you go to bed."

17

5. to begin to cook or heat something
transitive, separable

"Could you please put the kettle on?"

"I'm going to put on a pot of pasta."

common sentence: "Put this on." (Wear this object because it is suitable for the current weather conditions or occasion. Possible options: your hat, your jacket, your rain boots, your shirt, your dress, your suit, etc.)

Take off

1. to remove, especially something you are wearing
transitive, separable

"Take off your coat. It's hot in here."

"Please take your shoes off before entering the room."

"Take that picture off the wall."

"My mom believes that people should take their hat off when they enter someone's house."

2. to leave a place, often suddenly
intransitive
common extensions: take off at/after/before a particular time, or with someone

"She took off right after dinner."

"What time are you planning to take off?"

3. the act of a plane leaving the ground and starting to fly
intransitive
common extensions: take off at/on/in a particular time or period

"We have to hurry. Our plane takes off in an hour."

"What time does your flight take off?"

4. to suddenly become popular or successful
intransitive

"His career has really taken off since his last movie."

"An electric hammer is a terrible idea. It will never take off!"

5. to obtain time off; to take a vacation or a break
transitive, separable (usually separated: take time off)

"Moein has been stressed at work lately. He should take some time off."

"Brenda took off a year to travel after she finished high school."

common sentence: "It'll never take off." (That plan/invention/ song/etc. will never gain enough momentum to become popular.)

Pick up

1. to lift something or someone from a surface
transitive, separable
common extension: pick up something from a surface

"Pick up your toys!"

"Pick your socks up from the floor."

"Pick up your school bag. It's dragging behind you."

"Did you just pick that up from the floor and eat it? Gross!"

2. to get something or someone from a specific place, usually in a car
transitive, separable
common extensions: pick someone up at/on/in a particular time/ day/period of time/etc., or from/at a particular place

"Who used to pick you up from school when you were a kid?"

"I need to pick up some bread from the grocery store on my way home."

3. to acquire a skill or idea easily and over a period of time

transitive, separable

"She picked up the piano when she was seven."

"I've been trying to pick up Italian for a long time, but it's been difficult."

4. to talk to someone with the intention of getting them romantically or sexually interested in you

transitive, separable
common extensions: pick someone up at a place

"Someone tried to pick me up at work yesterday."

"He's always trying to pick up girls at the mall. It's kind of pathetic."

5. to acquire an illness from someone or something

transitive, separable
common extension: pick an illness up from someone

"Did you pick up a cold this weekend? You sound a bit sick."

"I'm pretty sure I picked the flu up from my kids."

common sentence: "Could you pick up some milk on the way home?" (Could you go to the store and buy some milk on your way to our house? A common request made by people you live with. The item to be purchased could be anything - bread, butter, eggs, juice, etc.)

Put down

1. to lower something or someone, usually onto a surface

transitive, separable
common extensions: put something down on/in a particular location

"You can put down your bag in the corner."

"Could you put down your phone and just listen to me?"

"I put the groceries down on the kitchen table."

"Put the gun down!"

2. to criticize someone and make them feel bad, usually in front of other people
transitive, separable

"He always puts her down in front of their friends."

"Why do you put down Francis so much?"

3. to write a note or piece of information on paper (also: write down)
transitive, separable

"Could you put down your contact information at the top of the page?"

"I put all of my mom's recipes down in a notebook."

4. to make a partial payment for something
transitive, separable
common extension: put money down towards something

"You have to put down a deposit before buying the fridge."

"We put down an extra three thousand dollars towards our mortgage last year."

5. to euthanize/kill an animal because it's old, sick, dangerous, etc.
transitive, separable

"We had to put our dog down last week."

"I don't want to think about putting down our cat, but she's been feeling sick a lot lately."

common sentence: "You can put it down over there." (You can place it there. Said to someone who is carrying something.)

Drop off

1. to deliver something or someone to a specific place, often in a vehicle

transitive, separable
common extension: drop someone/something off at a particular time and/or location

"Could you drop me off at work tomorrow morning?"

"I need to drop off some things at my sister's place."

"Did you drop off the check at the bank like I asked you to?"

"Just drop off the keys in my mailbox on your way home."

2. to decrease in quantity or intensity (slang intensifier: drop/fall off a cliff)

intransitive

"Their profits have really dropped off a cliff this quarter."

"Her interest in the project is dropping off."

3. to start falling asleep; to begin to sleep

intransitive
common extension: drop off to sleep

"Sorry, I missed that part of the movie. I must have dropped off to sleep."

"Make this presentation more exciting before the audience drops off."

common sentence: "I'll drop it off later." (I'll deliver it later. A common promise. The "it" can be anything: a bag, a book, a laptop, etc.)

Lesson 4

come in, get out, go back, come back, give back

Come in
1. to enter a room, building, etc.
intransitive

"Please come in. It's cold outside."

"Sorry for disturbing you. May I come in?"

"Take off your boots before you come in."

"She came in with four bags of groceries."

2. to appear or arrive at work
intransitive
common extensions: come in at/on/in a particular time/day/period of time/etc.

"Rita came in late this morning."

"Serge just texted me. He's not coming in today."

3. when a product arrives and/or becomes available at a store, it comes in
intransitive
common extensions: come in at/on/in a particular time or period

"Has the new issue of Batman come in yet?"

"When is the next shipment expected to come in?"

4. when news or information becomes available, it comes in
intransitive
common extensions: come in at/on/in a particular time/day/period

of time/etc., or on a particular media platform

"An update to the story just came in on Twitter."

"This news came in two hours ago. How come nobody told me sooner?"

5. **when money is deposited into your bank account, such as income from a job, the money comes in**
intransitive
common extensions: come in at/on/in a particular time or period

"The money finally came in this morning." (it came into my account)

"We can't afford the tickets right now. We're waiting for some money to come in."

common sentence: "Please come in." (Imperative used to invite someone into your home/office/room/etc.)

Get out

1. **to leave, exit, or escape a place or (usually bad) situation**
intransitive
common extension: get out of a place or situation

"Get out of here!"

"He's been in prison for five years. How many more until he gets out?"

"She's in a bad relationship. She needs to get out."

"Please get out of the car."

2. **to make or help someone leave, exit, or escape a place or (usually bad) situation**
transitive, must be separated (get someone out of a place or situation)

"Get him out of my house right now!"

"She helped get me out of a really bad situation."

3. to leave your house and enjoy yourself

transitive or intransitive (usually intransitive), must be separated if transitive (get someone out)

"My new job doesn't allow me to get out much."

"You need to get out more."

4. to remove something from a bag, container, etc.

transitive, separable
common extensions: get something out of somewhere

"Please open your backpacks and get out your homework."

"Get that candy out of your mouth!"

5. when information that is meant to be secret becomes known by many people, the information gets out

transitive, separable

"Make sure this information doesn't get out."

"The news of the company closure just got out this morning, but it's spreading fast."

common sentence: "Get out of here!" (Leave now! This is also used as a reply when someone says something that is surprising or unbelievable. Example: "You won a million dollars? Get out of here!")

Go back

1. to return to a place, person, job, situation, etc.

intransitive
common extension: go back to a place, person, job, situation, etc.

"You've been away from home for a long time. When are you going back?"

"Cesar has been talking about going back to school."

"I had to go back to the house because I had forgotten my wallet."

"How many times are you going to go back to her?"

2. **to return to a topic of conversation (go back to a topic)**
intransitive

"Let's go back to the discussion about affordable housing."

"During the meeting, we kept going back to the cost of the project."

3. **if two or more people have known each other for a length of time, they go back for that length of time**
transitive

"How long do you and Roger go back?"

"We go back at least twenty years."

common sentence: "We go back a long time." (We have known each other for a long time. Usually said about an old friend or colleague.)

Come back

1. **to return to or from a place, person, job, situation, etc.**
intransitive
common extensions: come back to/from a place, or at/on/in a time/ day/period of time/etc.

"Make sure you come back before 11 o'clock."

"Derrick's coming back to work tomorrow. He's been sick for a couple of days."

"Merida came back from vacation yesterday."

"Leave now and never come back. I never want to see you again."

2. **to start to exist again**
intransitive

"The pain in my back is coming back again."

"Her cancer hasn't come back in seven years, so we're all very relieved."

3. **to become fashionable or popular again (common: come back into style/fashion)**

intransitive

"Reggae is coming back in a big way."

"Bell bottom jeans are coming back into style."

4. **to recover from a bad situation, especially in sports**

intransitive
common extension: come back from something

"I can't believe Man U came back after being down by 3 goals."

"I'm going to come back from this injury and be stronger than ever."

5. **to react or reply to someone in a strong and/or clear way**

intransitive
common extension: come back with something

"I asked him a hard question and he came back with a good answer."

"He got punched in the face and came back with an uppercut!"

common sentence: "Come back!" (An imperative commanding someone to return. Often said angrily or desperately, but can be neutral.)

Give back

1. to return something to someone

transitive, separable
common extension: give something back to someone

"Give it back! It's not yours!"

"You can borrow my pen, but please give it back when you're done."

"Have you ever given back a gift that you didn't want?"

"Did Brandon ever give you the book back?"

2. **if you do something for a person, community, etc. to show gratitude for something they did for you, you "give back" to that person or community**

transitive or intransitive, separable
common extension: give back to someone or some place

"This community has given me a lot. I want to give back to it."

"You always took advantage of his kindness, but you never gave back."

3. **to return an emotion or feeling to someone that he/she had stopped feeling**

transitive, separable (common: give someone back something)

"Doing yoga has given me back my confidence."

"She's been sad for a long time. It will take a lot to get back her love of life."

Lesson 5

clean up, tidy up, use up, put away, put back

Clean up

1. to make something or some place clean or neat
transitive or intransitive, separable

"I need to clean up my room. It's a disaster."

"Could you clean the table up, please?"

"Max! Clean up this mess this instant!"

"I stayed home and cleaned up my basement this weekend."

2. to clean someone who is dirty, or to make someone neat and presentable who looks disorganized
transitive, separable (usually separated: clean someone up)

"Get in the shower and clean yourself up. You smell like a pig farm!"

"Your brother can't go to the wedding with that beard and those clothes. Could you help clean him up a bit?"

3. to make free from crime, corruption, and/or unacceptable behaviour
transitive, separable

"The new Prime Minister has really cleaned up parliament."

"The entire police department needs to be cleaned up."

4. to make a large profit or to get a lot of money
intransitive
common extension: clean up at a place or game

"I cleaned up at the casino last night."

"Wow! Looks like you really cleaned up at the BINGO tournament!"

common sentence: "Clean up your act." (Imperative telling someone to improve their behaviour, presentation, etc.)

Tidy up

1. to tidy or make tidy; to put things in their proper place so that everything is neat
transitive or intransitive, separable

"Tidy up the living room! Your aunt will be here in twenty minutes."

"I'm going to tidy my office up a bit."

"This place is a mess. He needs to tidy up more often."

"Don't forget to tidy up the kitchen counter when you're done cooking."

2. to make changes to something in order to improve it
transitive or intransitive, separable

"Could you tidy up this Excel document? The information is a little confusing."

"If we can tidy up this part of the policy, I think it will look much better to our clients."

common sentence: "Could you tidy this up?" (Could you make this area neat and tidy? Also: Could you make some small changes to make this look more presentable? Could refer to a document, presentation, etc.)

Use up

1. to exhaust/use something completely
transitive, separable

"We've used up all of the shelf space in our kitchen."

"Be careful not to use your allowance up all in one day."

"You've used up all my patience and now I'm mad."

"Who used up all of the shampoo?"

2. to exhaust something after repeated use (also: wear out)
transitive, separable

"Martin used up his new boots in just two months."

"Your bike needs new tires. These ones have been used up."

Put away

1. to put something in an appropriate or pre-designated place
transitive, separable
common extensions: put something away in/on a location

"Could you help me put the groceries away?"

"Put away your books, please. It's time to start the test."

"Why haven't you put your toys away yet? I told you to stop playing ten minutes ago."

"The dishwasher is done. I'm going to put the clean dishes away."

2. to eat or drink a quantity of something
transitive, separable

"I can put away two beers in thirty seconds."

"He's secretly been putting extra desserts away before bed."

3. to save an amount of money
transitive, separable
"I try to put a bit of money away every month. You never know when you're going to need it."

"My parents try to put away at least fifteen percent of their income into savings each month."

4. to be put into a prison or mental health facility
transitive, separable
common extensions: put away for a period of time, or for a particular reason

"He was put away for first degree murder."

"The judge put her away into a mental health facility because she was a danger to society."

5. to score a goal in a sport that has a net, basket, or other target for a ball, puck, etc.
transitive, separable

"She put three goals away against the Swedish national team!"

"How many goals did he put away last season?"

common sentence: "Put it away." (Put it where it's supposed to go. This imperative is also used when you don't want a person to use something or to have it present. Examples: "Why do you have a gun?! Put it away!" "You don't need to take out your wallet. Put it away. I'm paying today.")

Put back

1. to return something to a former and designated place
transitive, separable
common extensions: put something back in/on a location

"Who forgot to put the milk back in the fridge?"

"Put your money back in your wallet. I'm going to pay today."

"I told her that she needs to put back her toys into her toy box before getting any candy."

"It's taking me forever to put back all of these books."

2. to postpone to a later time or date (also: push back, put off)
transitive, separable
common extensions: put a scheduled event back until a specific time, or by a specific amount of time

"Could we put the meeting back by thirty minutes? I'm going to be late."

"The game had to be put back two hours because of rain."

3. to delay, push back, or impede progress

transitive, separable

"The new government has put the country back at least twenty years."

"The project won't be done on time. We were put back by unexpected delays."

4. to move time back on a clock, watch, or video

transitive, separable
common extension: put something back by a specific amount of time

"Don't forget to put your clocks back an hour this weekend."

"Could you put back the video by a few seconds and press pause?"

common sentence: "Put it back." (Return it to the place you got it from. Another example: "Put it back when you're done with it.")

Lesson 6

get along/on, take care of, look up to, run into, put up with

Get along (US) / Get on (UK)

1. to have a good relationship with someone

intransitive
common extension: get along/on with someone

"Do you get along with your dad?"

"My sister and I don't really get along."

"We've been getting on well with each other so far."

"I should introduce you to June. I think the two of you would really get along."

2. to make progress with something; to keep doing something (also, more common: come along)

intransitive

"How's your project getting along?"

"We're getting along well with our spring cleaning."

common sentence: "Can't we all just get along?" (Usually said in a joking manner, but could be genuine.)

Take care of

1. to be responsible for something; to deal with or handle something

transitive, inseparable

"Who's going to take care of the food for Adriana's surprise party?"

"Did you take care of your passport renewal like you said you would?"

"Bridget's taking care of the wedding invitations."

"I'll take care of washing the dishes if you'll take care of the laundry."

2. to be responsible for someone's or something's well being; to keep someone or something safe/ in good condition (also: look after)
transitive, inseparable

"My grandmother had to take care of nine kids!"

"You can borrow the book, but please make sure to take care of it."

3. to pay for something
transitive, inseparable

"Alan was generous and took care of the bill."

"Who's going to take care of the extra fees?"

common sentence: "I'll take care of it." (I'll handle it / I'll deal with the situation.)

Look up to

1. to respect and admire someone or a group (usually someone you know)
transitive, inseparable

"She never had anyone to look up to as a kid."

"I look up to anyone who can make something out of nothing."

"Who did you look up to when you were growing up?"

"Many of today's heavy metal bands look up to Metallica."

common sentence: "I look up to him/her/my dad/my mom/etc." (I admire this person.)

Run into

1. to collide or crash into something or someone (by car, bike, bus, train, or other form of transportation)

transitive, separable (when separated, list the subject's vehicle in the middle)

"He was drunk and ran his car into a tree."

"Did you see the news story about the bus that accidentally ran into an office building?"

"I ran my bike into a car."

"Slow down before you run into someone!"

2. to meet someone by chance (usually an old friend, a colleague, someone you know) (also: bump into)

transitive, inseparable

"I ran into my high school math teacher at the grocery store today."

"Enjoy the concert! Maybe we'll run into each other after the show."

3. to come against or to experience an unexpected problem or difficulty

transitive, inseparable

"I'm running into difficulties trying to set up my online banking account."

"They thought the project would be easy, but they've been running into a lot of problems."

common sentence: "Guess who I ran into today/yesterday/this morning/etc." (Guess who I met by chance.)

Put up with

1. to tolerate someone or something

transitive, inseparable

"I'm not going to put up with your lying anymore."

"Zakia has been putting up with her mother's criticism all of her life."

"I could never live in Manhattan. I wouldn't be able to put up with the traffic."

"The weather's been pretty bad lately, but we've been putting up with it."

common sentence: "How/Why do you put up with him/her/them/ etc.?" (I don't understand how or why you tolerate that person.)

Lesson 7

check out, try out, try on, pick out, show off

Check out

1. to look at, examine, or give your attention to someone or something to make a judgment about them/it

transitive, separable

"Check out my new bike."

"The doctor checked me out and said everything was fine."

"Hey Bryan, could you check this computer out for me? It's acting funny."

"If you're interested in architecture, you should check out the Art Deco district in Miami."

2. to consume or sample a piece of media (series, movie, album, song, video, video game, book, etc.)

transitive, separable

"Have you checked out the new Zelda game yet?"

"Check this song out. I think you'll like it."

3. to sample or participate in an activity, a location, an event, etc.

transitive, separable

"We're going to check the Van Gogh exhibit out this weekend."

"We really want to check out the new Vietnamese restaurant downtown."

4. to leave a hotel after staying there for at least one night

intransitive
common extension: check out of a hotel

"What time do we have to check out tomorrow?"

"I hate checking out of that hotel. They make everything so complicated."

5. to borrow a book from a library

transitive, separable

"How many books are we allowed to check out at one time?"

"Excuse me, sir. You have to check that out at the front desk."

common sentence: "Check it out!" (Look at this/that! Also, sample/examine/participate in this/that! A common casual imperative.)

Try out

1. to test someone or something to see if they're/ it's suitable for your purposes; to test someone or something in order to make a judgment about them/it (similar: check out)

transitive, separable

"I'm trying out a new exercise routine to improve my energy level."

"How do you know you don't like lentil soup if you've never tried it out?"

"We're trying out a new HR management software at work."

"We've tried out three different people for this job, and none of them were the right fit."

2. to go through a test to determine whether or not you're suitable to join a team, act in a movie, etc. (usually for performers: athletes, actors, etc.)
intransitive
common extension: try out for something

"The theatre company is looking for a good dancer. You should try out."

"Hundreds of athletes tried out for Norway's Olympic team."

common sentence: "Try it out!" (Test it! Try it!)

Try on

1. to put clothing on to see if it fits or if it looks nice
transitive, separable

"I hate trying clothes on at the mall."

"She didn't try on the dress when she bought it; now she has to return it."

"I think this hat might suit you. Why don't you try it on?"

"He's been trying on shoes for an hour already. He still hasn't found a good pair."

2. to try or test something to see if it's suitable (this meaning is figurative and means to try something on as if it were clothing)
transitive, separable

"I think this phone would suit you better. Why don't you try it on?"

"You want to wake up? Try this coffee on for size."

common sentence: "Try this on for size!" (Try this on! This often refers to clothing, but could be used in other contexts. Example: "You enjoy rock music? Try this on for size!" (the speaker then puts on a rock song))

Pick out

1. to select something or someone from a group
transitive, separable

"I hate picking my clothes out in the morning."

"Have you picked out what you're going to wear to the wedding?"

"We need to pick out a landscaping company."

"They've been trying to pick out a house for over four months now."

2. to identify someone or something from a group
transitive, separable

"Part two of the test is multiple choice. You have to pick the right answer out from the options given."

"Marcus had to go to the police department and pick out the guy who robbed him."

common sentence: "Who picked out your clothes this morning?" (Usually said in a joking manner if someone is dressed unattractively.)

Show off

1. to show something that you are proud of
transitive, separable

"Dorothy is showing off her new haircut."

"Bob's been showing off his new phone to everyone today."

"I never liked showing off my possessions."

"It's rude to show off your wealth in public."

2. **to try to impress other people by talking about or displaying your skills; to want to draw attention to yourself because of this**

transitive, separable

"He's good at piano, but he likes to show off a little too much."

"You're being too modest about your talent. You should show it off a bit more!"

common sentence: "Stop showing off." (Stop trying to impress others or to draw attention to yourself with your talent/skill. Can also be used in a joking manner.)

Lesson 8

find out, look over, look up, look into, come across

Find out

1. to discover or learn something that you didn't know
transitive or intransitive, separable

"I found out that my boyfriend was cheating on me."

"When are we going to find out who got the job?"

"She finally found the truth out about her mother."

"How did you find out about this place? It's great!"

2. to discover that someone has been doing something dishonest (find someone out)
transitive, separable

"She was a great computer hacker, but cyber security eventually found her out."

"If they're not careful, they're going to be found out by the police."

common sentence: "How did you find out about this/that/it/etc.?" (How did you discover or learn about this/that/it/etc.?)

Look over

1. to check, examine, review, or investigate something or someone, usually quickly (similar in some contexts: check out)
transitive, separable

"The detective is looking over the evidence."

"You should have a mechanic look your car over. It doesn't sound good."

"I've almost finished my essay. I just need to look it over one more time."

"The autopsy didn't reveal anything strange. They looked over his body multiple times."

common sentence: "I'll look it over and get back to you." (I'll review it and talk to you about it when I'm done.)

Look up

1. to search for something or someone in a list or database (physical or electronic/online)
transitive, separable

"Have you looked up his address yet?"

"Could you look up the meaning of the word 'terse' for me?"

"I don't know the answer to that question. Give me a moment to look it up online."

"I'm going to look up what there is to do downtown this weekend."

2. to show signs of improvement; to be getting better (usually used in the progressive tenses)
transitive, inseparable

"He's been in the hospital for a week, but the situation is looking up."

"The most recent financial analysis shows that things are looking up for our company."

3. to search for someone's contact information in order to make contact with them
transitive, separable

"Thanks for looking me up! Did you want to get together this weekend?"

"I'm so glad I looked him up on social media. We had an awesome time together."

common sentence: "Things are looking up." (The situation is getting better / There are signs that things are improving.)

Look into

1. to investigate or examine carefully; to consider
transitive, inseparable

"We're looking into getting a new car."

"Have you looked into alternative medicine for your knee problems?"

"I've started looking into the stock market to see if I can make some extra money."

"In the end, the printer model we looked into wasn't very good."

common sentence: "I'll look into it/this/that/etc." (I'll investigate, examine, or consider it/this/that carefully.)

Come across

1. to find or see something or someone by chance (a friend, money, a news story online, etc.) (also: run across; do not confuse with "run into")
transitive, inseparable

"I came across an interesting job advertisement online."

"We came across a homeless man playing the guitar on the subway."

"She told me she came across a twenty dollar bill in the parking lot!"

"You can expect to come across a lot of interesting costumes at Comic Con."

2. to give a particular impression of yourself with your words and/or actions
intransitive
common extension: come across as

"I want to read my speech to you to see how it comes across to an audience."

"Great speech! You came across as an expert on the subject."

3. **for emotions or ideas be expressed and received in a clear way; to be understood**

intransitive

"Your confidence really came across during your presentation."

"Her love of animals came across well in the video."

common sentence: "You're coming across a little strong." (I'm receiving your information in a negative way because of your high level of intensity.)

Lesson 9

look forward to, put off, call off, write down, hold on

Look forward to

1. to anticipate something with pleasure; to be happy and excited about something in the future

transitive, inseparable

"I've been looking forward to this trip for a long time."

"Are you looking forward to Neil Gaiman's new book?"

"Mirielle is looking forward to meeting you."

"I looked forward to visiting my grandma every weekend when I was a kid."

common sentence: "I'm looking forward to it." (I'm anticipating it with pleasure. The "it" could be anything: a movie, a book, an event, a meeting, an experience, a vacation, a video game, an announcement, etc.)

Put off

1. to delay/postpone something; to arrange to do something at a later time

transitive, separable
common extensions: put off by an amount of time, or until a future time

"Cathy has put off our meeting twice now. I feel like she doesn't respect my time."

"I'm too tired to do the dishes now. I'll put them off until tomorrow."

"I can't believe I'm going to have to put off my own wedding!"

"Sorry, but could we put our date off until Thursday night? I have a family emergency."

2. to make you dislike or stop liking something or someone

transitive, must be separated in active form (put someone off)
common extension: be put off by something or someone

"The last election put me off politics completely."

"The date was going great until dinner; I was put off by his chewing."

3. to make it more difficult or less attractive for you to do something (very similar to meaning 2 in some contexts)

transitive, must be separated in active form (put someone off)
common extension: be put off by something

"The length of the book has always put me off."

"She was excited about the job, but the low salary put her off."

4. to deactivate something (see also, more common: turn off)

transitive, separable

"Could you put the lights off in the bedroom, please?"

"Don't forget to put off the stove."

common sentence: "Don't put off until tomorrow what you can do today." (This is a famous proverb. It simply means "Don't procrastinate.")

Call off

1. to cancel an event/a meeting/etc., either one that is in progress or that is scheduled to happen in the future

transitive, separable

"Would you mind if we called our meeting off? I have a lot of work I need to do."

"I have to call off my dental appointment."

"They called off the game in the second half due to bad weather."

"The skiing trip got called off because there wasn't enough snow on the mountain."

2. to order an animal or person to desist; to order away
transitive, separable

"Call off your dog before he hurts someone!"

"The chief of police called off his officers once the criminal had been secured."

common sentence: "Let's call the whole thing off." (Let's cancel the entire planned or in-progress event/meeting/etc. This is also the name of a famous song written by George and Ira Gershwin. It has been sung by Louis Armstrong and Ella Fitzgerald, among others.)

Write down

1. to write; to take note of something (also: take down, type down)
transitive, separable
common extension: write something down at/on/in a location

"I wrote down the address."

"She wrote down all of her passwords in a notebook."

"You should have written his number down."

"Please write down your name, address, and telephone number at the bottom of the page."

common sentence: "Write it down." (Write it so you won't forget it and/or because it's important.)

Hold on

1. to hold; to keep your hand on or around something for safekeeping, in order to prevent it from falling, or to support yourself
intransitive
common extension: hold on to something (for an amount of time)

"Could you hold on to my phone for a minute?"

"I thought he would let go of the ball after he was tackled, but he held on."

"Hold on tight! It's going to be a bumpy ride!"

"My brother is holding on to my board game collection until I get back from vacation."

2. **to wait (commonly used as an imperative) (also: hang on)**
intransitive
common extension: hold on for a period of time

"Hold on for five more minutes, okay?"

"Hold on! We're on our way!"

3. **if you tell someone to stop talking while they're in the middle of saying something, you tell them to hold on, usually to clarify their idea or because you want them to listen and/or think**
intransitive

"Hold on a sec. What did you just say?"

"I tried telling him to hold on, but he just kept talking."

4. **to persevere and manage to be successful despite great difficulties/problems/odds/ challenges/etc.**
intransitive

"It was a close game, but they held on for the win in the end."

"If you hold on long enough, I'm sure you'll get that promotion eventually."

common sentence: "Hold on as long as you can." (Keep waiting or persevering for as long as you can.)

Lesson 10

get rid of, throw away, throw out, take out, cut down

Get rid of

1. to discard or give something away; to do away with something or someone; to free yourself from something or someone (similar in some contexts: throw away and throw out)

transitive, inseparable

"I'm considering getting rid of my entire comic book collection."

"Terrence is a terrible friend. You need to get rid of him."

"Could you get rid of all the old newspapers by the bed?"

"They had to get rid of their couch because it was too old."

common sentence: "Get rid of it." (Discard it and/or free yourself of it.)

Throw away

1. to discard; to get rid of something you no longer need (also: throw out)

transitive, separable

"My dad never throws anything away."

"Did you throw away the receipt?"

"Throwing stuff away can be kind of therapeutic."

"I never keep instruction manuals; I always throw them away."

2. **to waste something, like an opportunity, instead of using it; to discard in a foolish way**
transitive, separable

"I can't believe you threw away the chance to act in a movie!"

"Don't throw your life away."

common sentence: "I never throw anything away." (I never discard anything.)

Throw out

1. **to discard; to get rid of something you no longer need (also: throw away)**
transitive, separable

"Why did you throw those cookies out? They were still good."

"Did you throw out the box like I asked you to?"

"They're throwing out all of their old toys."

"Don't throw anything out without asking me!"

2. **to use force to make someone leave a place or group/club**
transitive, separable

"The security guard threw him out of the store because he refused to leave."

"He got thrown out of the air force because of his bad attitude."

3. **if someone in a position of power discards something official (a proposal, a legal case, etc.), they throw it out**
transitive, separable

"The judge threw the case out because there wasn't enough evidence."

"My boss threw out my proposal for a new staff kitchen because the project would be too expensive."

common sentence: "Throw it away." (Discard it because it's not useful.)

Take out

1. to extract or remove something from a bag, wallet, etc.
transitive, separable
common extension: take something out of somewhere

"Could you take some chicken out of the freezer?"

"Take the cake out of the oven before it burns."

"Take your school books out of your backpack."

"She's taking out a tube of lipstick from her purse."

2. to take or bring something or someone outside
transitive, separable

"I'm going to take out the garbage."

"Could you take the baby out for a walk?"

3. to invite and take someone somewhere and pay for them
transitive, separable
common extension: take someone out for something

"My husband took me out for breakfast. It was nice."

"You look a little down. Let me take you out for lunch."

4. to obtain specific financial services by fulfilling certain conditions
transitive, separable

"We took out a loan from the bank."

"I've never taken out a life insurance policy."

5. to kill or injure someone badly
transitive, separable

"I'm afraid that the mafia is going to take him out."

"Ouch! The goalie was just taken out by their striker!"

common sentence: "Take that out of my face." (Remove that from my line of sight because I don't want to see it, or because it's annoying me.)

Cut down

1. **to reduce the amount of something, often a damaging habit or something done or used in excess (spending, eating, drinking, smoking, etc.)**
transitive or intransitive, separable
common extension: cut down on something

"My mom has cut down the amount of sugar in her diet."

"We need to cut down the amount of pollution in major cities."

"I can't go out this weekend. I need to cut down on my spending."

"He used to drink six beers per day, but he has cut down."

2. **to make something shorter; to reduce the length of something (usually the length of time or the length of a piece of writing, video, etc.)**
transitive, separable
common extension: cut something down by an amount

"We enjoyed the movie, but we agreed the studio should have cut it down by at least fifteen minutes."

"Your essay was good, but you could have cut it down to make it even better."

3. **to cut through the trunk of a tree so that the tree falls down**
transitive, separable

"They haven't stopped cutting down trees in the amazon."

"This tree is rotten on the inside and needs to be cut down."

4. **if you criticize someone so that they realize they are not as talented or important as they think they are, you "cut them down to size;" to make someone humble**

"He's arrogant and needs to be cut down to size."

"Being in the military really cut me down to size."

common sentence: "No thanks. I'm trying to cut down." (Used to refuse an offer of something that you are trying to reduce the use or consumption of, such as coffee, smoking, drinking, chocolate, etc.)

Lesson 11

run out, give away, break down, clean out, put out

Run out

1. to use all of something until there's nothing left (also: use up, be out)

intransitive, inseparable
common extension: run out of something

"I'm running out of patience." (my patience is almost at its limit)

"I need a new pen. This one has run out of ink." (I have used all the ink)

"They can still tie the game, but time is running out!"
(almost finished)

"The car is almost out of gas. Stop at the next station to fill up."

2. to stop being valid or legal (a license, a contract, document, etc.)

intransitive

"His contract ran out and he signed with another league."
(context: athlete)

"I need to renew my driver's license. This one runs out next month."

3. to chase someone away or make them leave a place, usually a town or city

transitive, must be separated (run someone out of somewhere)

"The police ran him out of town."

"The security guard ran her out of the mall."

common sentence: "We're running out of time." (We don't have much time remaining.)

Give away

1. to give something to someone for free, often because you don't use it anymore
transitive, separable

"Her travel agency has been giving away trips to Hawaii!"

"Are you going to keep all those books or give them away?"

"Too many people just give their lives away to a company."

"You haven't watched these DVDs in years. Just give them away."

2. to allow an opponent to have an advantage, by chance or on purpose
transitive, separable

"We played chess on the weekend, and he was giving away important places on the board as if he had never played the game before."

"Our army was foolish to give the eastern mountains away to the enemy."

3. to reveal secret information or someone's true nature/identity
transitive, separable

"Nice costume, but your eyebrows totally give your identity away."

"He gave away our strategy to the opposition!"

4. to present a bride to her partner in a wedding ceremony, traditionally by her father
transitive, separable

"I'm not ready to give my little girl away!"

"I think the idea of a father giving away his daughter is too old-fashioned."

common sentence: "I gave it away." (I gave it to someone or some place for free. Usually said because you no longer needed something.)

Break down

1. to stop functioning (an electronic device, a machine, a car, etc.)
intransitive

"Our washing machine keeps breaking down."

"His car broke down on the side of the highway."

"My phone keeps breaking down. I've had to restart it three times today."

"This printer is garbage. It breaks down almost every single day!"

2. to lose your composure and start crying
intransitive

"I'm sorry for breaking down in front of you yesterday. Thank you for listening to me."

"At the end of the movie, we both broke down and cried."

3. to destroy a structure or obstacle
transitive, separable

"The police are going to break that door down any second!"

"The building manager wants this wall completely broken down."

4. to challenge social expectations, ideas, barriers, rules, or laws
transitive, separable

"Venus Williams has been breaking down gender barriers since she started playing tennis."

"I've been trying to break down these tired old laws for years now."

5. to reduce something to its individual parts; to explain something step by step (a plan, an argument)

transitive, separable
common extension: break something down into chunks/pieces

"I don't understand what you're saying. Could you break your points down a little more?"

"Let's break down the plan one step at a time and then talk about it."

common sentence: "Break it down for me." (Explain it step by step for me. A request to explain a plan, an idea, etc.)

Clean out

1. to take everything out of an enclosed space and/ or clean that space thoroughly

transitive, separable

"You'd better clean out your closet soon. It's starting to smell."

"We usually clean out the fridge at least once every six months."

"I'm going to clean out the guest room this weekend."

"You should really clean that drawer out. It's full of junk."

2. to take all of someone's money or valuables

transitive, separable

"I got totally cleaned out at the poker table."

"Cheryl really cleaned him out in the divorce."

3. to take all of a place's goods, valuables, or possessions, often in a way that is not legal

transitive, separable

"The police cleaned out the apartment but couldn't find any evidence."

"Someone cleaned our living room out over the weekend. They took the TV, the laptop - everything!"

common sentence: "Clean out your closet." (Empty your closet, get rid of what you don't need, and make it tidy.)

Put out

1. to extinguish (a fire, a flashlight, an emotion)
transitive, separable

"Put the fire out before you come back into the cabin."
(context: camping)

"Put your flashlight out! You're going to make me blind!"

"Rob's got some great advice on putting out one's anger."

"The power's back on. We can put all the candles out now."
(also: blow out)

2. to make news or an announcement known to a lot of people
transitive, separable

"Microsoft just put their sales numbers out for the past year."

"The liberal party is expected to put out a statement on the matter this afternoon."

3. to place something that is needed in a place where it is ready to be used
transitive, separable

"Dinner's almost ready. Could you put the utensils out?"

"We just need to put out some promotional pamphlets, and then our booth will be ready for the exhibition."

4. to cause problems for somebody by asking them to do something for you
transitive, must be separated (put someone out)

"I hate to put you out like this, but could you give me a ride to the airport?"

"She's done a lot for you already. Don't put her out any further."

5. to defeat a team in a competition so that they are no longer playing in it (also: knock out)

transitive, separable
common extension: put someone out of something

"Bayern Munich put Arsenal out of the Champions League."

"Do you really think that an eighth place team has a chance of knocking out a first place team?"

common sentence: "Put it out." (For fire: Extinguish it. For an item: Place it where it can be used, or place it outside.)

Lesson 12

point out, phone up, bring up, leave out, call on

Point out

1. **to call someone's attention to something; to point to something in order to show it (an object, a fact, a mistake, a direction, etc.)**

transitive, separable

"During the meeting, she pointed out that the company was losing money."

"I'd like to point out that I'm the only one here who arrived on time."

"My history teacher pointed all of my mistakes out in front of the class."

"I don't know where that is on a map. Could you point it out for me?"

common sentence: "Thanks for pointing that out." (Thanks for showing that, telling me that, and/or adding that piece of information to the discussion.)

Phone up

1. **to phone someone**
   (same: call up, ring up, hit up (slang))

transitive, separable

"You should call me up some time."

"I've been trying to phone him up for an hour, but he hasn't answered."

"I'm going to call the phone company up tomorrow. I think they made a mistake on my bill."

"Someone stole your credit card? Phone up the card company and cancel your card right away."

common sentence: "Phone/Call/Ring them up."
(Call them. A suggestion to call someone/someplace/etc.)

Bring up

1. to mention or introduce a point or topic in a conversation, email, etc.

transitive, separable

"Her research paper brought up some interesting points about endangered species."

"The golden rule of conversation with strangers is never to bring up religion or politics."

"If you're so upset about the new policy, why didn't you bring it up at the meeting?"

"Trent always brings up topics that no one cares about."

2. to raise a child or children until they are adults

transitive, separable

"My grandmother brought six children up on her own."

"Who brought you up?"

3. to be raised in a particular place, religion, or with particular attitudes

transitive, separable
common extension: bring someone up in a place

"My parents brought us up in Vancouver."

"She was brought up believing she was better than everyone else."

4. to vomit or cough up

transitive, separable

"Jenna's cat brings up a hairball at least once per week."

"Please stop talking about toilets. It's going to bring my lunch up."

common sentence: "I'll bring it up next time." (I'll mention it at the next meeting, during our next conversation, etc.)

Leave out

1. to omit something or someone in a story, conversation, speech, essay, activity, official document, etc.

transitive, separable

"Why did you leave out your address on this form?"

"Don't leave out any important details in your testimony."

"My brother always lied to our parents and left details out of his stories."

"When I was a kid, I was always left out of games in the schoolyard."

2. to place and leave something in an open space or outdoors

transitive, separable

"Did you leave the cat out last night?"

"Sorry about the smell. I accidentally left the fish out overnight."

common sentence: "Leave it out." (Omit it. Leave that detail out of your story, speech, essay, explanation, document, etc.)

Call on

1. to ask someone to recite, say, or do something publicly

transitive, inseparable
common extension: call on someone to do something

"The court would now like to call on the defendant."

"I'm always nervous when I get called on to speak in class."

"I'm now going to call on our president, Mike Mignola, to present our latest advertising campaign."

"Why didn't you call on him to make a statement?"

2. **to make a particular quality appear in oneself, usually with great effort**

transitive, inseparable

"I had to call on all of my strength to survive that situation."

"She called on her power of persuasion to negotiate her contract."

common sentence: "I'd like to call on (person's name)." (I'd like to ask this person to speak to the group. Usually said in a formal context.)

Lesson 13

go on, put up, take down, fill out, fill up

Go on

1. to continue doing something or to continue happening as before

intransitive
common extension: go on until a particular time, or for an amount of time

"The conversation went on for two hours."

"We should go on studying."

"How much longer does this movie go on for?"

"Sorry for the disturbance. You can now go on with your presentation."

2. to happen

intransitive

"What's going on here?"

"I don't know what's going on."

3. to start doing a particular activity or to start being in a particular state (ex. to go on vacation, go on a cruise, go on a trip, go on an exercise routine, go on a diet, go on sale, go on special)

transitive, inseparable

"I'll only buy it if it goes on sale."

"Don't go on a diet. Diets don't work."

4. **to start taking a particular medicine, drug, vitamin, etc. (opposite: go off)**

transitive, inseparable

"The doctor says I need to go on anti-depression medication."

"He was clean until he started going on cocaine again last week."

5. **to start doing or saying something again after a pause**

intransitive
common extension: go on with something

"The game went on after the rain stopped."

"Go on with your presentation. I'm sorry for interrupting you."

6. **if a light or device starts working, it goes on (similar: turn on, come on) (opposite: go off)**

intransitive

"I turned the key and the engine went on"

"The lights just went on in the next room. Did you turn them on?"

common sentence: "Go on." (Continue talking, walking, or doing what you were doing. This imperative is often used to encourage someone, but can be used sarcastically. "Wow, what an interesting story. Please do go on.")

Put up

1. **to place or fix something to a wall, board, etc.**

transitive, separable
common extension: put something up at/on/in a location

"You really ought to put that picture up in your room."

"Administration put up a new job posting in the staff kitchen."

"When did you put that poster up?"

"They're putting up new advertisements in the store windows."

2. to build; to erect

transitive, separable

"Have you seen all of the new condos they've put up downtown?"

"The police put up a bunch of barricades around the crime scene."

3. to raise the price of something

transitive, separable

"Gas stations are always putting up their prices."

"We don't shop there anymore because they put their prices up too high."

4. to provide or supply

transitive, separable

"Jerry's parents put ten thousand dollars up for his wedding!"

"Do you think they'll put up a good fight?" (context: a boxing match)

5. to accommodate or be accommodated, including providing or being provided a place to sleep (usually by friends or family) (put someone up)

transitive, must be separated
common extension: put someone up for a period of time

"We visited Chicago last month. We have friends there who put us up for a few nights."

"If you need a place to stay, I can put you up for a night. I have a guest room."

6. **to make something available for purchase or acquisition**

transitive, separable
common extension: put something up for sale

"They put their house up for sale last month."

"Have you thought about putting it up for donation?"

common sentence: "I put it up for sale." (I made it available for purchase. Usually a house, car, or an item that you advertise in a public place, on a sales website, etc.)

Take down

1. **to remove something from a high place, web page, bulletin board, etc.**

transitive, separable
common extension: take something down from somewhere

"After their breakup, Harriette took down all of their old photos."

"Would you mind taking down the statue that's on top of that bookshelf?"

"The news story was immediately taken down from the site."

"The president's controversial post was taken down."

2. **to dismantle or remove a structure**

transitive, separable

"I can't believe they took down the statue in the park."

"Police took down the barricades."

3. **to cause someone or something to fall as a result of violence**

transitive, separable

"The defender took down the striker."

"And he takes him down with just one punch! What a quick fight!"

4. to write or note down something
transitive, separable

"Did you take down everything the professor said?"

"Do you have a pen handy? Here, take down my number."

common sentence: "Could you take it/that down?" (Could you remove that from the wall, the shelf, the website, etc.?)

Fill out
1. to complete a form
transitive, separable

"Please fill out the bottom half of this form."

"She still hasn't filled her college application out yet."

"If you'd like to make an official complaint, please fill out an official complaint form."

"I hate applying for insurance. You have to fill so many forms out!"

2. to grow in size; to become rounder or fuller
intransitive, inseparable

"His physique has really filled out since high school."

"Most couples tend to fill out a bit after getting married."

common sentence: "You need to fill out a form/an application/ etc." (You need to complete a form/an application, etc. to apply for that service, account, and/or be considered for that position.)

Fill up
1. to fill something completely (a car with gas, a bottle, a room, etc.)
transitive or intransitive, separable
common extension: fill something up with something

"Why did you fill up this drawer with so much junk?"

"The car's almost out of gas. Can we fill the tank up at the next stop?"

"Five minutes before the movie started, the theatre filled up."

"Don't put it in that box. It's already filled up."

2. to eat something so you are no longer hungry

transitive or intransitive, separable
common extension: fill up on a particular food

"We shouldn't fill up on bread, or we won't have room for the main meal."

"My mom's food always fills me up."

common sentence: "Fill 'er up." (Imperative asking someone to fill a container or area completely. Usually a car's gas tank, but can be used to talk about filling a bottle, a cup, a glass, a bowl, etc.)

Lesson 14

show up, come over, stay in, stay up, wait on

Show up
1. to appear at a place and/or time
intransitive
common extension: show up at a particular place and/or time

"How many people showed up for the performance last night?"

"Eva always shows up late for work."

"The party starts at six o'clock, but you can show up earlier if you want."

"I searched for her address online, but no information showed up."

2. to be visible
intransitive

"This is an old picture, so the background doesn't show up very well."

"Sharpen your pencil. Your writing isn't showing up on the page."

3. to do something that makes someone feel embarrassed and/or foolish, while making the doer feel superior
transitive, separable (usually separated: show someone up)
common extension: be shown up by someone

"I can't believe you were shown up by a little boy!"

"You thought his goal was impressive? Get ready because I'm about to show him up."

common sentence: "When should I show up?" (When should I arrive?)

Come over

1. to visit someone; to go to where someone is
intransitive
common extension: come over to a place, or for something

"I'm at the library. You should come over so we can study together."

"What time should we come over to your place?"

"Wait for me in the theatre lobby. I'm coming over right now."

"You're in big trouble. Come over here this instant."

2. to overwhelm someone with a particular emotion
transitive, inseparable (come over someone)

"I looked at the ocean and a feeling of deep calm came over me."

"I'm sorry for yelling at you. I don't know what came over me."

3. to travel from one country and settle in another
intransitive
common extension: come over from a place, or in a year/decade/century

"My grandmother came over from Ukraine in the 1960s. My family has lived in Canada ever since then."

"I've been trying to get my family to come over here for a long time, but the immigration process has been difficult."

4. to give a particular impression of yourself with your words and/or actions (more common: come across)
intransitive, usually followed by an adverb or adjective
common extension: come over as

"Your email came over a little aggressive."

"I'm sorry for coming over as angry as I did."

common sentence: "Do you want to come over?" (Do you want to come to where I am? Usually an offer to visit one's home. The person offering does not have to be at their home when making the offer. A time qualifier is also often given, such as "Do you want to cover over tonight/later/after dinner/this weekend/etc.?")

Stay in

1. to stay in your home; to stay home because you don't want to or can't leave

intransitive

"We stayed in all weekend."

"I'm a bit worried about Clarissa. She's been staying in a lot lately."

"Sorry, I can't go out tonight. I need to stay in and study."

"I'm not going to do anything special tonight. Just stay in and watch TV."

common sentence: "I feel like staying in." (I don't want to leave my house. Often used with a time qualifier, such as "I feel like staying in tonight/today/this weekend/etc.")

Stay up

1. to remain awake; to not go to bed

intransitive
common extensions: stay up until a particular time, or for a period of time

"Millions of people stayed up to watch the gold medal final."

"What time did you stay up until last night?"

"We stayed up with our friends until the sun came up the next morning."

"Rebecca stayed up until two in the morning to finish her essay."

common sentence: "How late did you stay up last night?" (Another way of asking "What time did you go to bed?" Usually asked when the person looks tired or has already mentioned that they had a late night.)

Wait on

1. to serve someone (as a waiter, waitress, attendant, servant, etc.)

transitive, inseparable

"We were waited on by a very polite waitress."

"I've never had to wait on anybody."

"The Queen is waited on by dozens of private servers and attendants."

"His wife waits on him as if she were a slave. It's embarrassing."

2. to wait for a particular thing, event, person, etc. to arrive (also, more common: wait for)
transitive, inseparable

"I'm waiting on the decision from my job interview."

"We've been waiting on the band for over forty-five minutes."

common sentence: "She waits on him hand and foot." (This is an idiom meaning "She attends to his needs like a servant/slave." This is not usually complimentary towards the subject, but is usually said because you feel bad for the subject who is acting like a servant/slave.)

Lesson 15

drop by, hang up, do over, read over, blow up

Drop by

1. to visit someone or somewhere without an appointment, and/or for a short time (often followed by a location) (also: stop by)
transitive, inseparable

"Can we drop by the bank on the way home?"

"Drop by my office before you leave work today."

"Feel free to drop by any time after school. I'll be home all evening."

"Zack says he dropped by your place this morning, but you weren't there."

common sentence: "When should I drop by?" (What time should I visit?)

Hang up

1. to put on a hook/clothes hanger
transitive, separable

"You can hang your coat up in the front closet."

"Here, I'll hang up your jacket."

"Where can I hang up my sweater?"

"Could you hang this up for me?"

2. to end a phone conversation
transitive or intransitive, separable
common extension: hang up on someone

"Sorry about that. I hung the phone up by accident."

"Have you ever hung up the phone on someone in anger?"

3. **to stop doing a particular sport or activity after a long period/career by figuratively putting away/hanging up an object connected to that activity**
transitive, separable

"She hung up her skates after winning 5 Olympic medals."

"You're a forty-five-year-old boxer. Don't you think it's time to hang your gloves up?"

common sentence: "I'm going to hang up now." (I'm going to end the phone conversation now. A common context for this is telling someone on video chat that you're going to end the conversation so they're not surprised when the connection suddenly ends.)

Do over

1. **to repeat a task/job/test from the beginning; to do again, usually because you didn't do a good job the first time**
transitive, separable

"The professor allowed her to do the test over."

"This is a lazy report. Do it over and submit it to me by Friday."

"Sorry, that wasn't a good start. Could I do it over?" (context: a music student talking to their instructor)

"I wish I could do over my final year of high school."

2. **to renovate or redecorate**
transitive, separable

"We just did over our kitchen. We're going to do over our basement next."

"I think we should do the bathroom over. What do you think?"

common sentence: "If you could do it all over again, would you?" (Would you do it again if you had the chance? Usually said to make a person think about past mistakes.)

Read over

1. to read and quickly examine a text to get a general idea of what it's about (also: look over)

transitive, separable

"Did you read over the instructions before putting this bookshelf together?"

"I haven't had a chance to read the policy over in great detail yet."

"Chris is reading over some resumes today. We need to hire a new clerk."

"Is there a way we can read over the rules at home?"

common sentence: "Read it/this over and let me know what you think." (Read this and give me your opinion on it. Could be said to a work colleague whom you wish to read over an email that you are going to send.)

Blow up

1. to explode

transitive or intransitive, separable

"I can't believe they blew up a hospital."

"The goal of the game is to blow your enemy's base up."

"The plane went down after one of its electrical panels blew up."

"The bomb squad defused the bomb before it blew up."

2. to lose one's temper

intransitive
common extension: blow up at someone

"I wouldn't go into his office right now if I were you. He's ready to blow up."

"My mom rarely blew up at me when I was a kid."

3. to make an image or document bigger
transitive, separable

"I can't see what this document says. Could you blow it up a bit?"

"The designer thought the image on the poster looked too small, so he blew it up."

4. to become popular or increase in importance
intransitive

"The Beatles blew up in America after appearing on the Ed Sullivan show."

"With the right marketing, this product could really blow up."

5. to inflate (usually a balloon or a tire)
transitive, separable

"Do you need any help blowing balloons up for the birthday party?"

"Your rear driver's side tire looks like it needs to be blown up a bit."

common sentence: "I hope it doesn't blow up in your face." (An idiomatic sentence which means "I hope it doesn't have drastically negative effects that impact you personally." Usually said to someone who has described something they are doing or planning to do which has a degree of risk.)

Lesson 16

make up, come up with, hand in, catch on, grow up

Make up

1. to invent something (a story, idea, excuse, etc.)
transitive, separable

"I swear I'm not making it up! I really saw a ghost!"

"Don't listen to anything he says. He's always making up weird stories."

"I'm tired of you making up excuses."

"I wish I knew how she makes up such amazing stories."

2. to be part of and to form something (common passive: be made up of)
transitive, inseparable

"Canada, the United States, and Mexico make up most of North America."

"Water is made up of hydrogen and oxygen."

3. to compensate for lost work and time; to do something extra today because you missed something in the past
transitive, separable

"I need to make some hours up at work. I missed a lot during my vacation."

"The prof is letting Jacob make up his final exam because he had a family emergency on the original date of the test."

4. to become friends or partners again after a fight or disagreement

intransitive, inseparable

"You're still mad at Carol? I thought you two had already made up."

"Doug and I tried to make up, but we kept having problems afterwards."

5. to put on cosmetics or to have cosmetics put on you

transitive, separable (usually separated: make someone up)

"Hold on! I'm almost ready! I just need to make myself up a bit!"

"Have you seen Diana? Her cosmetician did a great job of making her up for the wedding."

common sentence: "I'll make it up to you." (I'll compensate you or return the favour later for the help you gave me or will give me. Usually a promise to show your gratitude for someone's help, but it can also be part of a desperate plea, such as, "Please help me! I swear I'll make it up to you!")

Come up with

1. to think of an idea or invention; to contribute a suggestion (an excuse, an idea, a plan, a reason) (similar in many contexts: make up)

transitive, inseparable

"Breanne always comes up with really creative solutions to problems."

"I need to come up with an excuse for why I can't go to the party."

"Does anyone know who came up with the air conditioner?"

"We've been trying to come up with a plan for the past two hours!"

2. to produce something when it's needed, usually money

transitive, inseparable

"How did you come up with a million dollars in three days?!"

"My insurance company says I need to come up with the money by Monday."

common sentence: "I'll come up with something." (I'll think of something. Usually said as a promise that one will think of a solution to a particular problem or situation.)

Hand in

1. **to submit something, such as homework, an essay, a test, etc. to a teacher or other authority figure**
transitive, separable

"Do you remember when we have to hand our essays in?"

"The prof said we can hand our work in online."

"Pencils down, everyone. Please hand in your tests."

"I lost twenty percent on the assignment because I handed it in late."

2. **to submit your written notice of resignation to your employer**
transitive, separable

"Did you hear about Karl? He handed in his resignation yesterday."

"I'm thinking about handing in my resignation if they don't increase my salary soon."

common sentence: "I'll hand it in tomorrow/this weekend/etc." (I'll submit it at this time.)

Catch on

1. **to become popular or well-known (a song, an idea, a fashion trend, an internet meme, a new word/expression)**
intransitive

"That new Bruno Mars song is really catching on. I keep hearing it."

"Her economic ideas are finally starting to catch on."

"I can't believe that trucker hats are catching on again. They're so ugly!"

"If I start using the word "cowabunga" around the office, do you think it'll catch on?"

2. to begin to understand, especially after a long time
intransitive
common extension: catch on to something

"Baseball is a little complicated, but I think I'm finally catching on to the rules."

"It took a while to explain our corporate strategy in a clear way, but I think everyone caught on eventually."

common sentence: "It's really catching on." (It's becoming popular and/or well-known.)

Grow up

1. to become an adult; to become bigger and/or taller
intransitive

"Your kids are growing up so quickly!"

"Growing up is hard for a lot of kids in this area."

"You won't grow up if you don't eat your vegetables."

"Some kids never want to grow up."

2. to become more mature; to think more sensibly
intransitive

"Dennis needs to grow up. He still acts like a kid."

"I think Roberta has grown up a lot this year."

3. used to discuss the place(s) and/or experiences one had as a child
intransitive

"Where did you grow up?"

"She grew up in a single-parent household."

common sentence: "Grow up!" (An imperative reaction that commands someone to stop acting like a child and start acting like a mature adult.)

Lesson 17

go through, get over, drop out, talk over, set up

Go through

1. **to experience or undergo something (often a difficult or painful event or period)**
transitive, inseparable

"Silvia just went through a really bad divorce."

"Have you ever gone through surgery?"

"Darek's going through a really rough time at work right now."

"Our downtown is going through a massive art revival."

2. **to use an amount or number of something; to consume (clothing items, food, electronic devices, machines, tissues) (similar: use up)**
transitive, inseparable

"I've gone through at least twelve phones in my lifetime."

"How many cups of coffee do you go through per day?"

3. **to search for something that's in a larger group of objects or in a particular space, or to put those things in order (email history, bills, closet, drawer, books, collections, etc.) (similar in some contexts: clean out)**
transitive, inseparable

"I need to go through my closet this weekend. It's a mess right now."

"We've gone through every drawer in the house, and we still haven't found our passports."

4. **to complete a routine, a series of actions, or a procedure in the way you normally do it (an exercise routine, steps in a process, a religious ritual, etc.)**
transitive, inseparable

"It usually takes me twenty minutes to go through my daily yoga routine."

"We'd already gone through the first three prayer rituals when you arrived."

5. **to be approved by a governing body and be put into law or policy (a government bill, a popular vote, a company policy, etc.)**
transitive, inseparable

"There were three rounds of discussions before the law went through."

"You should still be able to apply for your summer vacation. The new vacation policy hasn't gone through yet."

common sentence: "I'm going through a lot right now." (I'm experiencing a lot of difficulties and/or problems right now. Often refers to a person's mental health struggles in the middle of life events.)

Get over

1. **to recover from an illness, disappointment, or difficult time (a death in the family, the end of a relationship, etc.)**
transitive, inseparable

"Haven't you been trying to get over that cold for two weeks now?"

"He still hasn't gotten over his breakup with Vanessa."

"Roderick has never been able to get over the death of his son."

"How long does it usually take to get over the flu?"

2. to find a way to overcome a problem
transitive, inseparable

"If we can just get over this part of the project, the rest should be easy."

"We've got some major hurdles we need to get over." (idiomatic: "hurdles" refers to problems)

3. to do something just because you want it to be finished and/or want to start doing something else (get something over with)
transitive, must be separated

"I don't want to do this, but let's get it over with."

"He said he wasn't looking forward to his vacation and just wanted to get it over with."

4. to deliver a message to people and have them understand it
transitive, separable

"I think I got over the importance of this change in the meeting."

"They're trying to get over the idea that this is a safe place to work."

5. To be unable to overcome your surprise or shock at something
transitive, inseparable (common: can't get over something)

"I can't get over how much you've grown up since last year!"

"She couldn't get over how much her hometown had changed."

common sentence: "Get over it." (Overcome it and/or stop wasting your energy on it. Often said as an imperative to command someone to stop complaining about something or talking about something from the past that they were surprised by or felt hurt by, such as the end of a relationship, someone speaking negatively about them, failing a test, etc.)

Drop out

1. **to quit school before completing your diploma, degree, certificate, etc. (or to quit a class or program before completing it)**

intransitive
common extension: drop out of

"Mike dropped out of high school in grade ten."

"Chihiro told me she wants to drop out of the program."

"If you're not enjoying the class, why don't you drop out?"

"He's been talking about dropping out of college for a few months now."

2. **to stop participating in a race, competition, or activity with an end goal**

intransitive
common extension: drop out of

"She had to drop out of the race because she injured her leg while training."

"They dropped out of the competition as a result of a drug scandal."

3. **to stop participating in a group, a society, etc.**

intransitive
common extension: drop out of

"I wish I could drop out of this capitalist society."

"Our group needs you. Don't drop out."

common sentence: "I dropped out." (I quit the class/school/ program/competition/etc.)

Talk over

1. **to discuss something completely and honestly (similar: go over)**

transitive, separable

"Why don't you come over tonight so we can talk over the proposal?"

"I don't think talking it over again is going to solve anything."

"We talked it over for a long time, but we still couldn't agree on anything."

"Stop avoiding me. We need to talk this over and move on with our lives."

2. **to speak louder than someone when they're talking; to speak louder than something that is making noise (ex. a truck, a television, a radio, etc.)**
transitive, inseparable

"Can we go somewhere quiet? I can't talk over the music in this room."

"Ryan kept talking over everyone during the meeting. He was really rude."

common sentence: "Why don't we talk it over?" (Let's discuss the situation and review it in detail.)

Set up

1. **to arrange or create something**
transitive, separable

"We're keen to set up our business as soon as possible."

"Do you need any help with setting up your website?"

"We bought a TV sound system, but we don't know how to set it up."

"How long did it take you to set up your living room?"

2. **to place or build a temporary structure**
transitive, separable

"Welcome to the exhibition hall. You can set your booth up over there."

"The concert organizers did a bad job of setting up the protective barriers in front of the stage."

3. **to complete the required process in order to start a piece of machinery, an account, a video game, etc.**
transitive, separable

"I still need to set up my online account."

"Could you help me set up my printer?"

4. **to establish yourself in a new location or company**
transitive, separable

"They've been having a hard time getting set up in London."

"We're going to set the business up downtown."

5. **to put someone in a position where it seems like they have done something wrong, when they are actually innocent**
transitive, separable (usually separated: set someone up)

"I didn't do it! Someone must have set me up!"

"He says his uncle set him up and that the drugs weren't his."

common sentence: "Let's set it up." (Let's organize it and/ or arrange it in the expected order. Could refer to arranging something physical, such as a piece of furniture or a complex toy, but could also arranging plans to get together with someone.)

Lesson 18

take after, catch up, look down on, walk out, look after

Take after

1. to resemble someone in appearance, habits, interests, etc. (usually a family member, but can also be someone you know or someone famous)
transitive, inseparable

"In terms of looks, I would say Derek takes after his mother."

"Stop picking your nose. Don't take after your brother."

"Zelda's really into ballet. She's taking after her grandmother."

"He's trying to take after the Dalai Lama."

2. to take on the same profession as someone else (usually a family member or someone you know)
transitive, inseparable

"I took after my mother and became a nurse."

"They both took after their uncle and became mechanics."

common sentence: "He takes after his (someone he knows)." (He follows or resembles his mother, father, etc. in some way.)

Catch up

1. to go faster and reach someone or something that is also moving ahead of you
transitive, inseparable
common extensions: catch up to/with someone

"They're ten kilometers ahead of us. We'll never catch up."

"I've been trying to catch up to her for an hour, but she's just too fast."

"Lee left a minute ago. If you hurry, you might be able to catch up to him."

"He caught up with him in the final lap and won the race!"

2. to work and/or improve in order to reach the same standard as others
transitive, inseparable
common extensions: catch up to/with someone

"I missed two weeks of classes. I need to work hard to catch up with the other students."

"Jack's brother was always more successful than he was. Jack felt like he would never catch up to him."

3. if you catch up on something, you do something you have been neglecting or procrastinating on
transitive, inseparable

"I need to catch up on my schoolwork."

"We've got a lot of housework we need to catch up on."

4. if something catches up with you, you are forced to deal with something unpleasant that you have been avoiding or something that is inevitable because of your past or present actions
transitive, inseparable

"You might feel fine now, but eating all that junk food is going to catch up with you eventually."

"Rita's working seven days a week. I hope all that stress doesn't eventually catch up with her."

5. to meet and/or communicate with someone you haven't spoken to in a long time and to tell each other the latest news about your lives
transitive, inseparable

"I caught up with Mark this weekend. We hadn't seen each other in a year!"

"It's been a long time since we last talked. We should catch up some time."

common sentence: "We should catch up sometime." (We should meet casually sometime in the near future and talk about our lives. Often said to old friends or people we haven't seen in a long time.)

Look down on

1. **to think you are superior or more important than someone; to think someone doesn't deserve respect (idiom intensifier: look down your nose at someone)**
transitive, inseparable

"Don't look down on me."

"Marjorie's been looked down on her entire life."

"She's always looking down her nose at me."

"In war, soldiers are taught to look down on their enemies."

2. **to think something is not good enough for you**
transitive, inseparable

"She has always looked down on public schools."

"Why do you look down on fast food restaurants?"

common sentence: "Don't look down on him/her/them/etc." (Don't think you are better than him/her/them/etc.)

Walk out

1. **to abandon or leave someone or something (a romantic partner, family, teammates, an event, a gathering, etc.)**
transitive, inseparable
common extension: walk out on someone/something

"I'm thinking about walking out on Gerald."

"I can't believe he walked out on his family. He has three kids!"

"Do you want me to walk out on everything we have built over the last twenty years?"

"I walked out on the movie because it was terrible."

2. to abandon or desert something (a meeting, an opportunity, a job)

transitive, inseparable
common extension: walk out on something

"She walked out on the company after twelve years of service."

"If you leave now, you're walking out on the biggest opportunity of your entire life."

common sentence: "I walked out." (I left the place, event, person, or situation because I could no longer handle it/them.)

Look after

1. to take someone or something into your care, either for a long period of time or temporarily (children, pets, property) (also: take care of)

transitive, inseparable

"Who's going to look after your birds while you're away?"

"By the time he graduates, we'll have been looking after him for twenty-two years."

"I'm looking after my neighbor's house while he's on vacation."

"Robert doesn't look after his things. He always wears them out or breaks them."

2. to accept something as your responsibility (a task, housework, a bill)

transitive, inseparable

"I'll look after the dishes if you look after the laundry."

"Caroline's been looking after our finances for several years now."

common sentence: "Who looked after you as a kid?" (Who cared for you when you were a child?)

Lesson 19

break up, keep away, look in on, check up on, talk back

Break up

1. to end a relationship with someone
transitive or intransitive
common extension: break up with someone

"Diana broke up with Ted last week."

"Why did the two of you break up?"

"We broke up yesterday."

"Gerard broke up with me."

2. to separate or divide into several smaller parts, groups, etc.
transitive or intransitive, separable

"The country has been broken up into east and west."

"Let's break up this project into three different teams."

3. to bring an end to a gathering, meeting, or fight
transitive, separable

"The protest got broken up by the police."

"Break it up! Stop fighting!"

4. to not have good and consistent reception quality during a phone call, online conversation, online stream, etc.
intransitive (usually used in continuous)

"Sorry, your voice keeps breaking up. Could you repeat that?"

"The video stream is breaking up."

5. **to separate something (an area, period of time, activity...) so that it does not feel as large or long; to make an area, time, or activity more manageable and/or less redundant**

transitive, separable

"I like to break up my morning work routine with some exercise."

"The developers broke up the game with bonus levels that are completely different from the rest of the adventure."

common sentence: "Break it up!" (Stop fighting! This can also mean "Stop talking" if one directs it to a group that is discussing something and one wants them to stop.)

Keep away

1. **to remain at a distance or to avoid something or someone**

transitive or intransitive, separable
common extension: keep away from something/someone

"Keep away from the speakers if you don't want to damage your ears." (context: at a concert)

"I think you should keep away from Daria. She's a bad influence on you."

"The police instructed the crowd to keep away from the metal barrier."

"He needs to keep away from sugar because of his diabetes."

2. **to prevent somebody or something from going somewhere**

transitive, must be separated (keep someone away)
common extension: keep someone/something away from somewhere

"The high crime rate keeps me away from downtown."

"The flu kept Geraldine away from work for an entire week."

common sentence: "Keep that/him/her away from me." (Keep that/him/her at a distance from me. This can be used to show disgust, fear, or dislike of something or someone.)

Look in on

1. to visit someone to see how they're doing (similar or same in most contexts: check up on)
transitive, inseparable

"Would you mind looking in on the kids for me? They're in the living room."

"Could you look in on my dog when I'm on vacation?"

"Our camp counselor constantly looked in on us at night."

"You're my son! Of course I'm going to look in on you when you first move out."

common sentence: "Could you look in on him/her/them?" (Could you check and see how they are doing?)

Check up on

1. to investigate and see how someone or something is doing (similar or same in some contexts: look in on)
transitive, inseparable

"Could you check up on the kids? They're being really noisy upstairs."

"Would you mind checking up on the laundry? It should be done by now."

"Her mom has been checking up on her every day since she started college."

"I'm going to check up on the pasta. It's been cooking for around ten minutes now."

common sentence: "You don't need to check up on me so much." (I can take care of myself and I don't need you to make sure I'm okay so often. Often said by adolescents to their parents.)

Talk back

1. to answer someone impolitely (usually kids answering their parents)

intransitive
common extension: talk back to someone

"If you want to stay out of trouble, don't talk back."

"Jake! Don't talk back to your mother like that!"

"It's not polite to talk back to your parents."

"I always talked back to my teachers in high school, so I spent a lot of time in detention."

common sentence: "Don't talk back to me!" (Don't answer me with anger, rudeness, or impoliteness. Usually said by an angry parent to a child. For a stronger impression, one can also say "Don't you dare talk back to me!")

Lesson 20

keep up, get away with, look out, make out, pass out

Keep up

1. to maintain pace with someone or something
intransitive

"Slow down! I can't keep up with you!"

"I was shocked that he was able to keep up."

"She talks fast and is hard to keep up with in a conversation."

"The second place driver is keeping up with the leader."

2. to be able to follow and understand someone or something's speech, reasoning, structure, etc.
intransitive
common extension: keep up with someone/something

"Could you repeat that? I'm finding it difficult to keep up with your logic."

"This movie is really complex. You have to pay attention to keep up with it."

3. to continue to be in contact with someone
intransitive
common extension: keep up with someone

"Hey, have you kept up with Sheri since we graduated?"

"I feel bad that we haven't kept up with each other, you know?"

4. **to be aware of and follow current events, news, etc.**
intransitive
common extension: keep up with something

"Have you been keeping up with the Premier League this season?"

"I try to follow the news, but it's so hard to keep up."

5. **to continue to do something regularly (an exercise routine, a diet, a payment plan, etc.)**
intransitive
common extension: keep up with something

"I haven't been keeping up with my yoga classes."

"They cancelled his account because he couldn't keep up with his payments."

common sentence: "Try to keep up." (Try to keep the pace and keep going. Usually said as a friendly warning, but can also be used in a joking or rude manner, such as "We talked about that ten minutes ago. Try to keep up!")

Get away with

1. **to successfully do something bad without being punished or criticized for it**
transitive, inseparable

"A couple of guys got away with robbing the national bank."

"I can't believe she got away with it!"

"Did you really think you were going to get away with lying to me?"

"The government's been getting away with overtaxing people for too long!"

2. **to succeed in doing something without any bad results**
transitive, inseparable

"I've been working out a lot this week, so I can get away with eating a big bag of chips today."

"Drake got away with not studying for the test. He still got ninety percent!"

common sentence: "You'll never get away with it/this." (You won't be able to do it/this without getting caught and/or punished. Usually said to express doubt or disbelief towards the person who thinks his/her plan will work. Also a common line in many movies: "You'll never get away with this!" Response: "I already have.")

Look out

1. to be careful and pay attention; to anticipate/be ready for something or someone (same: watch out)
intransitive
common extension: look out for something/someone

"You have to look out for speed bumps when you're driving in this neighbourhood."

"Look out for that van!"

"Look out! You're going to crash!"

"Jackie worked there before. She said you have to look out for all of the liars who work there."

2. to take care of someone and make sure nothing bad happens to them (similar: take care of, look after, watch out for)
transitive, inseparable
common extension: look out for someone

"Thanks for looking out for me when I was a kid."

"Erica's been looking out for her little brother since they were kids."

3. to focus your attention on trying to find someone or something (look out for someone/something)
transitive, inseparable

"My dad said he's coming to pick us up now. Look out for a red van."

"Keep your eyes open and look out for the police in this neighbourhood."

common sentence: "Look out!" (Be careful! A common imperative and warning used in a dangerous situation. Also: "Watch out!")

Make out

1. to be able to hear, see, or decipher something that may be difficult to hear, see, or decipher
transitive, separable

"Sorry, I can't make out what you're saying. Can you speak a little louder?"

"I can't make out what it says at the bottom of this form."

"I've tried to catch the words to this song a million times, but I just can't make them out."

"Hey Jack, could you take a look at this email and tell me what you think it means? I'm having a hard time making it out."

2. to make a check payable to someone
transitive, separable
common extension: make out a check to someone

"Have you ever had to make out a check to a member of your family?"

"Okay, I've written down the amount on the check. Now who should I make it out to?"

3. to progress or perform
intransitive
common extension: make out with something

"How's Mahmoud making out with your homework?"

"I just talked to Brian in Mumbai. It sounds like he's making out okay over there."

4. to kiss passionately
transitive or intransitive, inseparable
common extension: make out with someone

"Don't lie to me, Daniel. Everyone saw you making out with Julie at her birthday party."

"What's the weirdest place you've ever made out with somebody?"

common sentence: "I can't make it out." (I can't see what it says or shows because it's not clear. This can also be used to say something is difficult to understand. Example: "I read Plato's Republic, but I couldn't make it out.")

Pass out

1. to distribute something to a group (same: hand out)

transitive, separable
common extension: pass out something to someone

"The teacher passed out the final exam papers to the students."

"I'm going to pass out our annual report at next week's meeting."

"Could you help me pass out these forms?"

"She said she's going to pass out the final results to everyone tomorrow."

2. to lose consciousness; to faint

transitive or intransitive, inseparable
common extension: pass out from something

"He didn't drink enough water and passed out from dehydration."

"The room was so crowded that she passed out from a lack of oxygen."

3. to go to sleep (slang)

intransitive
common extension: pass out on something

"What time did you pass out last night?"

"Do you mind if I pass out on the couch for a couple of hours?"

common sentence: "Could you help pass these out for me?" (Could you help me to distribute these forms/papers/etc. to the group? Often said by a teacher to their students, or by someone in a meeting or presentation.)

Index

About the Author

Alex Makar is a Polish-Canadian immigrant who has been teaching English in and out of classrooms since 2007. In 2009, he decided it would be a good idea to show his face to millions of people on YouTube and on engvid.com. He has not regretted this decision.

These days, Alex resides in the province of Quebec with his wife, two daughters, and pet bird, Totoro. When he's not answering grammar questions or trying to write books, Alex enjoys reading, watching movies, playing board games, collecting nerdy t-shirts, pretending to maintain a regular exercise routine, listening to music, and learning from his kids.

For more English learning resources, including free video lessons, go to:

EnglishAlex.com

Made in the USA
Monee, IL
27 October 2024

68755179R00066